SUMADE - PART 1

PURPOSE OF LIFE & OTHER INTERESTING THOUGHTS

SUMEDH G. M. DESHPANDE

To Sudha Murthy, for helping me cope with the loss of my

beloved grandmother

To Jyoti Teacher, for giving me the confidence to

showcase my work

To Shimoga Teacher, for keeping me tethered & focused

To Kalpana Ma'am, for giving me a second chance

To my family, for supporting me throughout my journey

To my friends & loved ones, for believing in me every step

of the way

To you, the reader, for giving my work an opportunity

Author's Note

Sumade - Part 1 is the first part of a series that captures the small yet powerful shifts I've made in my habits or my thought process that have made a lasting impact. The title itself reflects this journey, combining two essential ideas: 'Su', meaning "good" in Marathi, a tribute to my mother tongue and the foundation of my thought process; and "made", for the intentional steps I've taken towards growth.

These changes may seem minor, however they've created remarkable transformations in my life. Through this book, I hope to share my learnings with you, not as instructions, but as reflections, allowing you to absorb, question, and evolve in your own way. I want this book to enhance the dialouges we have with ourselves, creating a shared journey of self-discovery rather than a one-way conversation.

Sumade as a series is a continous exploration of self-improvement, aiming to become better versions of ourselves, with a focus on inner contentment - no matter where we are in life. Thank you for joining me on this path!

Contents

Acknowledgements

I owe immense gratitude to the people who stood by me as I brought this book to life. My heartfelt thanks go to my friends Anurag, Karan, Atul, Surabhi, Gauri, Arya and Harrshada, whose support fueled my journey as a writer. I am especially grateful to Maryam for her unawavering encouragement and faith in me.

To my family, I cannot thank you enough. My brother, Pratik Dada, has been a true beacon of hope. My parents, for their nurturing love, space, and the freedom they gave me to embrace my individuality. My sister-in-law Dilpreet, for her constant cheering and helping me find my way when course correction was needed. And finally, my niece Kyra, whose joy and laughter light up my days.

There are countless others who I would like to thank for being a part of this journey, I appreciate the love, support from each and everyone of you for making this dream a reality.

Preface

Dear Reader,

Thank you so much for taking the time to read my work. I am incredibly grateful for the opportunity to converse with you. I refer to this interaction as a conversation rather than a one-sided dialogue because that's how I envision the journey we'll embark on together as you explore my thoughts. My intention is to introduce you to these ideas and engage in a meaningful discussion—these are merely my views, not the absolute truth. I believe that by discussing these topics, we can uncover more dimensions of the truth.

Please feel free to reach out to me at theguywhosortawrites@gmail.com if you want to share your thoughts. I would absolutely love to hear what's on your mind.

This book is my attempt to bring to light some of the topics I believe should be discussed more broadly, whether it's about consent, breaking generational cycles, dealing with breakdowns, and much more. I look forward to our journey together as you turn these pages!

CHAPTER I

Purpose of Life

What do you think life is? What do you think is the purpose? Maybe we are just meant to be lost for the whole of it. Maybe we are supposed to create a path for ourselves, or maybe, just maybe, it is all too arbitrary. For me specifically, life is about finding what you love and doing what you love. Here's what I mean by that: Let's take a step back to put things in perspective. Right now, you are reading this very sentence. You are somewhere in your city, which itself is in a state of a country that stands tall on a continent situated on this planet. Think about the fact that this very planet is a part of the solar system and how the list goes on and on from there. When we look at our lives from a cosmic standpoint, how difficult do you find your problems? How difficult do you find it to do the task that you were supposed to do?

Don't get me wrong; the things that affect you are important, and the way you feel matters a lot, but as you do, there must be days when your brain is set to wonder what this universe has in store for you. In your life, you are the universe. You are the one who creates and destroys. You are the one who, when the time comes, fades away and is born again. So now that we have some perspective, let's talk about life again. In my opinion, or from whatever I've learned so far in life, there doesn't seem to be a point. Maybe trying to find your purpose can be the ultimate goal, but don't you feel that's too much of an effort? We are from a generation that is used to having answers one search away from the tip of our fingers, and now you are telling me that

I'll have to put effort into building my own self?

So is there another option? I'll tell you what I feel. I feel life is too pointless, and what you end up doing is the point. Maybe you have your own stance on our role in the universe. I'd love to talk to you about it someday, so do feel comfortable reaching out. Since this is more of a monologue, this is my stance: I feel we, as humans, were meant to progress, maybe into an intergalactic species and beyond. So whatever part we can play and whatever help we can offer to someone within our limits, I feel we should. You never know who might just need a gentle smile to fight off a horrible day. One good thought travels a thousand miles.

As far as your purpose goes, just think about the limited time we have at our disposal and the responsibilities we bear on our shoulders. When you take these two things into consideration and plan the things that you'd do for yourself, I believe that's your purpose. Don't stress over it too much; don't go into a panic. All I'm saying is that it can be whatever you want it to be. Think about the fact that the universe decided to go through the effort of the big bang, melting into planets that could be habitable, and setting up a whole civilization only so you could live this moment. Now, if someone or something put so much thought into your existence, maybe we could fight a bit harder. Maybe we could find time to do the things we love after all. Maybe we could spend time with our family. Remember, be mindfully consistent.

One of the things that helps me a lot is asking myself, "How?" There were a lot of times when I'd often ask myself the question, "Will I be able to do this?" And one day, when I started asking myself, "How will I do this?" the answers started pouring in. Ask yourself, as an extension of the universe, what is it that is stopping or holding you back? Spend time with your family, read that book, paint that sketch, or do one of the thousands and millions of things at your disposal. Just don't stop. Even if you feel you want to take some time off and spend some time alone, you have every right to. It's your universe; it's your story; you get to make these decisions to determine the course of your life. Sure, there are other factors involved, but remember that your reaction and your mindset to deal with a situation are all yours.

Someone once told me that life is fair because it's unfair to everyone. I believe that life is life, and we are we. We just have to do what we want to and believe in to achieve the things that we long to see. So maybe that's what life is all about. The confusion, the highs and lows, the love that you feel, and the pain that eats you inside. No matter what it is, remember that you are the universe, and the universe is you.

CHAPTER II

Parents & Loved Ones

Growing up, one of the things that always stood out to me was the role of our parents. I often wondered why my dad had to be like my dad, and the same was true for my mother. Is there something hardwired into them that makes them this way? I just couldn't understand where they were coming from. In my mind, it always worked on a simple basis: they are my parents, and they know what's best for my elder brother and me. They are the final deciding authority. It also stemmed from the other part of life where I believed adults, in general, knew the rationale behind their decisions.

As I grew older, I started noticing something different, something that made me question the foundation of my ideas. I believe all of us go through that phase when we stop seeing our mom and dad as our mother and father and see them as individuals. If not, then I'd highly recommend doing it. I used to always think, "Wow, my mom and dad are so strong and confident in whatever they do. I want to be like them." Wouldn't it be nice to know what to do when? Having that level of maturity was something I longed for. Little did I know the price at which they gained those skills.

If you ask for my simple take on the issue, it goes something like this: our generation has it a bit easier when it comes to lifestyle choices. Looking back, I realize that my parents had immense pressure on their shoulders. They had to get a job. They had to work around the clock. They had to always dedicate themselves to something or another. For them, it was about survival. They had other siblings to look after and their own family to care for, and they had to make sure there was always something to keep the stove burning in the household.

As opposed to that, my elder brother had to struggle a lot as well. When it finally comes to me, when it comes to these sets of responsibilities, I would say the pressure was a lot less than it was in their time. I had a lot of liberty in finding and searching for the things and domains I wanted to work in, which wasn't the same for them. This is where I see a vast difference arise. See, I'm with you when you talk about the exponential rise in competition, the fact that some of you must've suffered the parting from your parents, and even the fact that every generation has its own set of hurdles to deal with. I even understand that every family, goes through these cycles across the society and different stratas. Granted, all these things are true, but I want you to understand that we aren't working on binary logic here. I'm not talking about the idea that if I feel they had to struggle during their time when they were as old as I was, then it makes my struggles inferior to theirs. It's a discussion about whether we acknowledge their efforts as much as we acknowledge ours. Do we ever sit back and wonder, "This was the age when they took up the responsibility of their whole family; would I be able to do the same?" Is it a good thing or a bad thing that I don't have to? These are some of the questions I truly believe everyone must ask themselves.

You see, what I've noticed over the years is that when you are propelled into a life of decision-making with a very short window and a lot of pressure, you tend to lose your individuality. Maybe for some people, it works out, but for the rest—and the majority—this is my standpoint. How many of us know our parents as individuals? Do you know your mother's favorite song? What did she dream of when she was a child? How often do you sit with your father and ask him about how he spent his childhood days? What's their story, and what is it that they wanted to achieve as individuals?

Once I started having these conversations with both my parents, I realized how wrong my assumptions were about them. It had nothing to do with age and everything to do with the ability to bear the consequences of a decision. Practical experience does carry a lot of weight when you set out on the voyage of life. There is some truth in the criticism or nagging that they direct at us. I began to realize that they too had their own set of vulnerabilities, dreams, and aspirations. Just like that, the picture became a lot clearer. Behind the mirage of heroic mom and dad stood two individuals who just wanted to be heard. Who just wanted to tell their story and open up?

I know it won't be easy for everyone, but if you want to put in the effort and if you have the mental capacity to listen to them, I'd recommend doing that. If your feelings and desires are to be taken into account, then why not theirs? It's been a gradual process of all of us trying to figure out the rights and wrongs of our behavior while trying to be the best versions of ourselves. I feel that over time, we should have the maturity to sit down and have these discussions with them since they too want to voice themselves, tell us their story, and help us understand the extreme amount of effort that goes into the making of a parent.

CHAPTER III

Introspection

How often do you have a conversation with yourself? How often do you sit yourself down and ask what is wrong, what you need to work on, and most importantly, what has been on your mind all this time? In this hectic schedule of ours, try to find a couple of minutes to spend some time with yourself and understand what you are, or rather who you are, as an individual.

Introspection is extremely important. A lot of us tend to ignore it at its face value. We tend to find reasons not to have a conversation with ourselves. We try to run on autopilot because we know that if we actually sit ourselves down and try to engage in a conversation with ourselves, it's just the cue for all the floodgates to open. Everything that was kept at bay will come pouring down. Now, the question I have for you is, is it really that bad? It just might be. Don't get me wrong—I felt this way for quite a long time too. It's easier to avoid conversations when they're with yourself. You can always keep engaging in one activity or another, finding ways to keep yourself distracted. The only problem with this approach is that, on the surface, even if it's bright, sunny, and shiny, the storms that rage inside continue to brew, waiting to cause havoc. Sooner or later, in some form or another, it will definitely break out.

So where do we go from here? For the longest time, I did not want to have difficult conversations with myself. Why would I actively engage in conversations that make me uncomfortable? These conversations would be about my actions, mistakes I made, things I could have done better, my dreams, aspirations, and so on. Why would I try to think about these things? It just didn't feel right. What I began to notice as time went on is that it was much easier for me to listen to other people's feelings regarding the same set of topics, yet when it came to myself, I was always at odds with them. That's when I decided a change was needed.

On some level or another, I needed to try to engage in a conversation with myself because things were not working out. I began with small steps, which involved having conversations with myself and pretending to listen to my problems as if they were someone else's. I know, I know—it seems like a long route, and yet for some reason, that's how my mind functioned. Believe it or not, it worked. I found myself being more compassionate and understanding toward my problems. I tried to go out of my way and ask myself, "What is it that you want? What is it that you wish to achieve?"

Once I started having these conversations, I began to notice how I was as a person. What actions or habits of mine did I need to focus on? You see, if you can't be honest with yourself, how do you expect to be honest with others? If you can't acknowledge your own shortcomings, how do you plan on working on them? When you start diving deeper, you discover so much more. Try to be your friend. Try to dissociate yourself from you for a second and understand where you are coming from. Look at how far you've come. Look at how much progress you've made. If you can rejoice and clap for your friend's achievements, why not for your own?

Why not be happy about what you have accomplished over the years? Every hurdle, every tantrum, every single day when you thought, "This is it; this is my breaking point;

life beyond this will hold no value to me in any shape or form," and yet here you are, still in the ring, fighting to make things better.

This is your story. This is you, putting everything you've got on the line and making sure you do better with each passing day. Take a deep breath and just understand. It wasn't easy. It wasn't easy for any of us. Yet, you made it. I am proud of you, and you should be too. That doesn't make us perfect. It merely makes us human. This isn't a talk about how you should just accept yourself for who you are. Understand that, at some level or another, all of us are hypocrites. So use that—question yourself, ask yourself about your actions, try to find the correct path, and lead yourself to be a better version of you. You can't always hold things against yourself. You can't always judge the future based on the actions of the past. You need to give yourself the benefit of the doubt in some cases, and in some cases, you need to hold yourself accountable for your actions. Be a better friend to yourself. Take an active interest in your interests. Listen to your own laments. Cheer for yourself and drown in your sorrow from time to time. Just know that you'll be there for yourself. That you will be a better friend to yourself. Don't give up just yet. Your best is yet to come.

CHAPTER IV

Consent & People

Consent. We've all heard the word at some point in our lives. The sad truth is that we've all wished there were more people who understood what the word truly signifies. It's hard to imagine that seven letters can carry so many emotions—something that could have made many lives easier if people only knew what it meant. Before I dive into the topic, I want to acknowledge that this is a sensitive subject for many of us. You are not alone. It's beyond imagination what some of us have gone through, and yet we have to pretend for most of our lives as if nothing happened. This chapter, though it may be brief, is an effort to educate and inform readers, who will, at least for a moment, consider the magnitude of feelings attached to the word "Consent". So, before continuing, if you feel that this might be something you're not ready to read, discuss, or go through again, I advise you to move to the next chapter or take your time. There's no rush at all.

As for the remaining part, this needs to be out there. People need to understand. So, let's jump right into it. No one likes unwanted advances. At no point would someone willingly want to be touched inappropriately or against their wishes. If the people of the world understood these sentences, we wouldn't be in this situation. You've probably heard stories of people in your life talking about being touched inappropriately or leered at in an unpleasant way. Let me bring the topic to the limelight—it's not just stories. There are thousands of people around you who have gone through these moments. It's hard to believe, it's horrible to imagine, and yet, in a strange way, it's true. I wish it was easier, that we could sugarcoat it and erase it from existence, but that would be dismissing the ill actions of some people, and that can't be left unchecked. All the victims and the perpetrators are people we know: a friend, a relative, or even a stranger. There's no limit to where this behavior can seep in. Maybe the actions were innocent is a question that pops into everyone's mind, and yet we fail to understand the gravity of the situation.

If you ever find yourself in a situation where you have to gauge whether the actions were innocent or deliberate, take my word for it—assume they were not. Consider it your instincts telling you that something is wrong. Even if, as some people may have you believe, you are thinking too much or it's all in your head, the outcomes of assuming it to be deliberate and taking precautions accordingly outweigh those of considering them innocent. I know it feels wrong at every stage. Just because there are people out there who can't seem to wrap their heads around the concept that "no" means "no"—that it's not a challenge to be won—does not mean you should ignore your instincts. There are actual lives at stake. Not everything boils down to someone's wish and command. The world would be a much better place if people understood this. These are protocols we have to put into place because something needs to be done. We can't always keep people in the dark and expect them to understand a muddled world that never comes to light. At some point, we have to be strong and open up about these incidents.

For the vast majority, these things don't happen, and you never assume it has happened to someone close to you. We keep them in the shadows to protect the people we care about and to prevent them from worrying. The only way to truly protect them is to tell them the truth in your own way and at your own time. The fact of the matter is, the more we discuss and share these incidents with the people close to us, the more we'll understand and learn. Learn that "no" is not something that devalues you as a person. It means a thousand things, but not that. The best thing to do is to confirm with someone you're romantically interested in whether they are okay with your actions or what you plan on doing.

Trust me when I say this: at no point will you find that asking for your partner's consent is a turn-off. At no point will you find that a passionate, forced kiss or touch means more to them than you taking their feelings into account. You'd have their respect for considering their emotions. It's hard for some people, and it's worse for others when these things are overlooked. When we look at people as nothing but objects and things to conquer, something we can get away with, that's when we drift away from a sane society. We can't keep criticizing how messed up the world is without taking it upon ourselves to be more open—not to the whole world, but to the people you trust. There are people who have spent countless days and nights fighting to rid themselves of those images. They are like you and me, wanting not to let these events define who they are as individuals, yet it's a herculean task to separate it from themselves.

So yes, consent matters. The other side of the people who lead to these events are also people we know—a friend, a relative, or a human being. Left unchecked, we can't imagine the horrors that await us. Consent matters. Every single syllable of it. Every moment of it. Each and every second lived devoid of it has hampered a lifetime of moments for some people. Take it as your responsibility to educate yourself and those close to you. Make sure that you do your part. Sometimes you may have done things innocently—clear the air. Take responsibility for your actions. Even if you can't go back and change what you've done, you can always avoid repeating them in the future. Educate and eradicate.

CHAPTER V

Finding What You Love

One of the hardest things I've seen people struggle with is explaining what they love to do, whether it's their job, hobbies, or any other activity. I guess there's a part of us that attaches a lot of value to the word "love," and we want to save it for the very best thing that can happen to us—keeping it very sacred. When I had to decide what I wanted to do for myself or in terms of finding my passion, I had a hard time narrowing down the options. I say "options" because you can have more than one goal; you don't have to limit your ambitions to just a single target. You can have a variety of interests spread across technical, sports, creative fields, and so much more! Let that idea sink in.

Growing up, I had a rough idea of what I wanted to pursue and where I wanted to be, and life just kind of dragged me along the way. In my opinion, all of us should have—or do have—a natural heuristic, something that feels like a good direction to head towards. But how often do we actually take the time to sit down and truly listen to what our mind tells us? At every point in life, we should have the courage to ask ourselves, What is it that I want to do? I understand that we might not always have the luxury to act upon our desires, especially to the level we want, but there's always a start. If you don't begin, how will you critique your efforts and understand whether you actually like doing it or not? The idea is to build a foundation and then slowly build on top of it. We must start somewhere.

Sometimes, we assume we'd enjoy doing something, but when we finally have the chance, we lose all interest. That's the thing about people—they can change, and that's completely fine. You don't need to hold onto every piece of yourself. As time progresses, you have every right to change, modify, and work on your opinions and beliefs. That's the whole point of being human. If we don't change, how will we improve?

Over the last couple of years, when I've had the "passion/what you love to do" talk, I've noticed that a lot of people take a step back. It's the number one question you don't want to ask someone because they're one step away from an existential crisis. I feel that much of this comes from the fact that we are often pushed into things, and decision-making is not developed as a trait but rather as a situation-based execution talent that gets refined with time and exposure. When you run the majority of your life on autopilot, it can be a bit frightening to take the controls into your own hands. So tiny steps all the way.

The majority might think, "Only if there's a favorable condition, then I would act this way." Nothing wrong with it. There's always something about staying in the comfort zone in known environments that tends to restrict our true potential. That being said, there are those on the other side of the spectrum who have a clear understanding of what they want to do and what path they should follow to reach that goal. I was more in the middle, and if you ask me, a part of me still is. Like I said, people find it very difficult to either admit they don't know the whole story or that they don't want to discuss it. They would most likely just avoid the conversation altogether by shying away from the subject, which again is completely understandable.

I feel that, as people, we need to learn to say that we simply don't know something. Is it really that difficult? There are only three scenarios: either you know for sure that you like something, so that's a yes; you know for sure that you don't like something, so that's a no; or it's neither, and it's a maybe. This three-pronged way of looking at things has always helped me make a lot of decisions. When you find yourself in this position, it's always best to give it a chance and actually see whether you enjoy what you're doing. You'll always end up understanding better to what degree you like or don't like something; this will come handy in making boundaries. This is when your maybes become more definite yeses or noes. You do this by minimizing your lack of exposure to the field and figuring out how you feel about it. As humans, we have a gut feeling that tells us whether we are inclined toward a particular field or not. As time progresses, you can keep refining your approach, and sooner or later, you'll have your answers.

The way I decide what I want to do is very simple: ask yourself, What are the things that you enjoy doing? A lot of people think about their careers negatively, as just a means of survival. Yes, even if that's true, there are ways to improve. Add things to your plate that you enjoy. Like I said, it's a continuous process of finding yourself and discovering what you love doing. Start small—maybe you like organizing, maybe you like planning things to the dot, maybe you enjoy crunching numbers. It can be anything. Try to think about the things you enjoy and build your career around them. Don't do it the other way around. You have to understand that you'll never have 100% of the answer, but you'll always be one step closer to where you feel like you belong. The idea is that as your career progresses over time, you should be able to add more of the things you enjoy to your plate, as opposed to those that you don't.

Imagine someone asks you in the middle of the night to do a particular job or solve a particular business problem. If your reaction is wondering why you're doing it in the middle of the night, yet you're comfortable getting it done because it's something you don't mind doing, then that itself is a sign. It shouldn't be something that keeps you constantly on edge, yet it needs to be something that makes you want to do more. If the idea completely irks you, maybe you need to reconsider what you have been doing.

The truth is that there will never be a straight answer; life will always be a process of trial and error. But with each unexplored avenue, you'll eventually end up in the right neighborhood—the one where what you love actually resides.

CHAPTER VI

Habit of Building

If you're anything like me, you probably have tons of things you'd like to include in your daily life or work on. It could be something you want to learn, read, or even just exercise regularly. Yet, despite having the best intentions, you might find yourself unable to follow through. That's where discipline and habit formation come into play. It might seem easy to map it out in your mind, but putting it into practice can be quite challenging when the stage is all yours.

So, how do we go about it? What can we do to get there? Let's start by assessing the current situation. In today's world, we're used to having information at our fingertips. With the modern world progressing at an exponential speed, we've become too accustomed to quick results. Want to watch a cooking video? There are thousands of them on the internet. Want to read? There are tons of choices available that can be delivered to your doorstep. Given all this, why is it so difficult to form new habits? Maybe our attention spans have shortened? Maybe we've become too dependent on technology to give us constant reminders? Or maybe, just maybe, it feels like a futile mission. But don't worry—as ironic as it may seem, we are all creatures of habit.

You may have wondered during the lockdown how it was ever possible that you used to get up early every day and go to school or work, doing those activities day after day without even batting an eye. It's all about making it a habit. It requires patience and time. As daunting as it may seem, the process is actually quite simple. Simple, but not easy.

You need to start by creating a routine. Let's say you decide you want to exercise three times a week for half an hour each day. You've set your goal; now it's time to incorporate it into your routine. The moment you have an epiphany along these lines, you should act on it within the first 5 seconds. Plan when you'll do it, and then actually do it. If it comes down to it, start at that very instant. Even 5 minutes of effort counts. Now, every alternate day, try to meet those five minutes as a target. The first thing you need to do is build a pattern. Once you've established a pattern, you'll notice your body responding to it. After a few weeks, you might find yourself wondering why you haven't done it already. There will be times when you feel uneasy if you haven't exercised. You might even relapse and think it's all in vain. Spiraling is part of the process. Tiny steps are what you need to keep in mind. Once you've established a pattern, only then can you start optimizing it. You can introspect and think about how you can do better—where you can find more time, what you're doing right, what you're doing wrong, and what else you should be using your time for. These reflections will come naturally to you.

One of the most important things is that you need to be honest with yourself about these things. You need to have that honest conversation with yourself and figure out the time, effort, and energy to dedicate to your goal. This means your resolve and your purpose need to be stronger than your willingness to throw in the towel. You start with these tiny initiatives, and over time, with incremental consistency, you get better. I always looked at it as hey, I exercised zero minutes through the week, and now I am at a much better place. That, for me, is a win in itself. The idea is to move a bit further than your current self to a better self.

The bottom line of all of this is that you can only criticize and improve something if it's in front of you—if you're actually doing something in the first place. It can be tiresome to think, "There's no time in my hectic schedule," or "It's too cumbersome to try and exhaust myself even more." If that's the case, then meditate. The moment you get out of bed, meditate, and let your body relax for the first few minutes of your day. Once you realize how beneficial it is, you'll slowly start making it a part of your schedule.

There are so many things you can do with your time. These days, we often find ourselves mindlessly scrolling through our feeds, wondering where the time goes. There are so many things we can do, so many things we can learn, if only we could form the habit to do so. Learn to cook, go for a walk, read a book, explore new hobbies, exercise, meditate—do whatever you feel like doing. If it's relaxing and helps put your mind at ease, then do that as well. Just know that the tiny steps you take now will help you scale the mountains of the future.

CHAPTER VII

The Rat Race That Defines Us

You and I have always been competing—at least, that's what we've been told. And that's where the problem lies. Your skills have never been entirely your own; they've been shaped in comparison to someone else's set of skills. The issue with the rat race is that there is no end to it. There is no finish line. You'll have to keep going and going until you completely exhaust yourself. Even if you're ahead because of a head start, sooner or later, you'll find yourself trying to catch up to your peers.

Everyone is built differently. Everyone is intelligent in their own way. As individuals, we need to learn from all the life experiences and people we encounter. Life has always been the greatest teacher. When you learn to pay attention to the subtle lessons life offers, you'll do much better in the future. Think about this from a fundamental perspective: at every moment, you are compared to someone else. From the time you're a baby, it's about who started talking first, who rolled over first. In school, it's about who's better at extracurricular activities and who's better at studies. In life, it's about who's more successful, who's more likely to "make it," and so on. When will it stop? It won't. When will your life stop being about others and start being about you? You are you, aren't you? An individual with your own set of feelings and emotions.

Yes, comparison can help you understand how to improve yourself, but getting stuck in the limbo of feeling like you're not measuring up to others is unhealthy. So, learn about yourself. What are your wants? What makes you tick? What drives you? These are essential questions. The more you know about yourself, the less you'll care about the world's opinions.

There will come a time in your life when you wonder whether you've been left behind. Since the race is always on your mind, this is a natural feeling. But remember, everyone has their own journey. If you want to make comparisons, the short answer is: you can't. The fact is, even thinking "they did better" or "I did worse" depends on countless factors like their background, upbringing, health, and so on. Even siblings experience things differently. So, learn when to say, "No, this isn't for me. This is what I want; this is what I'm looking for, and this is what I will work toward." If you don't know what you want, you can experiment and find your way. Just don't mold your success metrics based merely on others' criticism. I am not saying don't take anyone's opinions into consideration; be open to criticism, especially from those you trust and who are close to you. The onus is on you to know whose opinion to take into consideration and value. There is always some truth in what these people say, but only from those who genuinely care about you. Listen to their words, but implement only what you believe is necessary.

Remember, you are constantly changing. You aren't the same person you were a minute ago. Some fundamental values will change over time, while others will change moment by moment. And that's okay. The entire human race has thrived on adaptability, so change when it's needed.

As for your peers, know that no one has it easy. Take this as an absolute truth. No one just stumbles upon success when they step out into the world. There are sacrifices behind every success that often go unseen. What meets the eye is only the perfect picture portrayed; there is no universal mantra for success. There are habits that can put you on the path to success, but it will still come with its own set of hurdles that you'll have to cross. So, understand that just because you feel your peers are ahead of you doesn't make it true. They have their own journey, and you have yours. Ask yourself where you want to be and work toward it. You'll have your own set of responsibilities to handle before you get there. It's already difficult enough for everyone that no one wants the burden of being considered lucky for their achievements. Yes, privilege exists, but it exists to some degree for all of us. The way this world works is if you succeed with your privilege, you were lucky, and if you don't, you were a fool. So, the sooner you stop paying heed to these things, the better.

Rejoice and cherish the achievements of your friends and loved ones. Learn the art of understanding yourself. You'll discover how wonderful it is to truly know the real you. If you don't have anything nice to say, remember it's okay to say nothing at all. You can never take back words spoken in the heat of emotion. So, help yourself and help your peers by being there in whatever capacity you can. Only then can we hope to escape this rat race.

CHAPTER VIII

Learning Through Life

All of us are here for a reason. Whether you believe it or not, your actions cause a ripple effect that you can't fully fathom. We all wonder about our place in the universe, but there is no definite answer. The easy thing to understand is that there are bigger forces at play, and all of our lives are interconnected in complex ways. One of the most essential things to learn early in life is that mistakes are inevitable. You will never know everything at any given moment. It takes time to learn how to make fewer mistakes, but the only way to do so is to make them.

Be a learner. Understand that life is the best teacher, and through its teachings, you will learn all the necessary things to fulfill your destiny. That's what I've always felt. We have the resources we need to power through our problems; all we need to do is think and show discipline. Consistency, consistency, and more consistency is key.

Everyone has their own share of intelligence to offer the universe. It may be something they've learned through the hardships of life, something taught by their parents or relatives, or something they discovered on their own. Be open to learning. Don't assume you know everything. Once you start understanding that there are people around you who know more than you do, you'll realize how infinite the process of learning is. The more you understand, the less you'll know.

This applies universally: you can be smart, but understand that you might not be the smartest person in the room. The ability to admit that you messed up without considering yourself a failure comes with practice. It comes from knowing your fundamentals, your beliefs, and the type of person you aspire to be. You can learn from anyone, regardless of their position in society. A sweeper who works day in and day out can teach you things that a class-A finance person might never fathom. Again, everyone has their own share of knowledge, so it goes both ways. Listen to everything, but implement only what you feel is essential. Don't disrespect or dismiss anyone's perspective based on their social standing.

This brings us to making mistakes. Let's consider a simple example: did you always know that if you keep your head wet for too long after playing in the rain, you might catch a cold? You were informed, but you didn't really think it was possible. Over time, you made your mistakes and developed your own understanding of how your body works. It's the same with mistakes—you'll know what you want to avoid only after you think it through and understand, in the first place, what it is that you want to avoid.

Another important aspect is how we perceive mistakes. They are not a reflection of your character. You were in a situation; you made a bad call, but that doesn't make you a bad person. It makes you human. So when correcting others, do it in the right way. Simply shouting or biting someone's head off won't get you the result you want.

Sometimes you have to be gentle; you have to be open and honest. In most cases, try not to misplace your anger. Correct people in the way you would correct a child. You might need to change your approach depending on the person, but know that belittling is not the right response. If someone isn't capable of handling the task assigned to them, that's something you'll learn over time. Competency is important, and understanding people's competency is also a skill. So if you feel unsure about your ability to perform a task, don't be afraid to reach out and ask for guidance. Learn how to do it on your own, and you'll become a better individual.

You will never possess all the knowledge that the universe holds. What you will have is the ability to understand what comes before you. So be open and respectful, change when necessary, and life will be an amazing ride.

CHAPTER IX

Break You Down

We've all been broken down. We've all had those moments where we felt like this was it. This is where it ends. This is my limit. We've all had those moments where we just felt like we couldn't take anything more. Yet, despite all that, here you are—fighting or trying to make your life better.

Breakdowns happen. You find yourself on your knees, lost and unsure of how you will continue. At that point, it's not just about one thing; it's everything. I've had moments when I just wanted to run into an open field and scream at the top of my voice out of sheer anguish—a cathartic scream to let go of all my emotions. What I've learned over time is that, as difficult as it might seem, this isn't the way. Sure, it can be part of the process, but you'll have to actively work on yourself to move forward. When the time comes, reach out—get help from your trusted circle, and talk it out. The problem with bottling up your emotions is that sometimes you run out of space. Sooner or later, there will be a downpour. When those floodgates open, everything—and I mean everything—comes pouring down. You might even find yourself misplacing your emotions because you don't know how to channel them properly.

It's hard being human. It's hard being you. No one has it easy. We're all in the same boat. Everyone is fighting some battle or another; it's just that we're oblivious to the wounds because most of us are great at hiding them. In these situations, you have to be honest and gentle with yourself. Sometimes you have to wait out the storm, and sometimes you have to sail into the sea, come what may. Do it on your own time. Understand that the things that broke you before will not continue to do so over time, as long as you give yourself the time to heal. Time is the best healer.

In some cases, you have to work on yourself. You have to ask yourself and others whom you trust how you can do better, and then work on it. Remember, it takes a big person to admit their shortcomings. It takes a lot of guts to be vulnerable. No one likes being in that position, yet sometimes the path to recovery is by doing just that. Cry if you have to. I don't know why we've defaced the act of crying. It's pure and simple. It shows that you cared. Isn't that why you're upset? Isn't that why you find yourself trembling with emotion, crying relentlessly even when you promised it was going to be for the last time? So take a few deep breaths. Sometimes, a few deep breaths can change everything. You will be fine. There will come a time in your life when you'll look back and be proud of the journey you've made up to that point.

Allow yourself to feel. Be honest with yourself. Don't hold things against yourself. If you can critique your mistakes, you can also advocate for your victories. Have faith in your potential and give yourself reasons to do so. The path to success is full of hurdles, and sometimes it's okay if your car breaks down along the way. You don't throw out your car. You don't curse it for being useless. You understand that it too has its limitations. If you drive it rough, if you don't take care of it, often it will lead to this point. You can always do better. The sooner you realize this, the better you will have it in the long run.

Break down so that you can build yourself up. Learn what gets to you and understand who you are as an individual. It's okay to set boundaries. Boundaries help us protect the things we love, especially if that thing is you. So just know, while it might seem dark and gloomy now, there will be better days—days when you will laugh and rejoice. Celebrate that you made it through.

CHAPTER X

What the World Has Done to You

It's difficult to think about where you want to go and how you want to get there. It's not easy having goals and navigating your way toward them when you have no clear idea of how they're even achievable. You can't work toward something you don't know—that's the problem. Let's just put it out there: none of us have it all figured out. So if you feel that someone has every aspect of their life figured out, let me take the opportunity to tell you that isn't the case. What you can know is the general direction you're supposed to head—a heuristic at best. Believe me when I say this: that's enough.

When you try to make life a series of programs or a journey where you have to reach from point A to point B, you tend to miss out on the opportunities you could stumble upon along the way. Keep in mind that with time, your choices can change, and your ambitions can change, which is natural. You are human, after all. In most cases, the general direction where you want to head will stay the same. Think about the kind of life you want and the routine you want, and then plan your life accordingly. It doesn't have to be a single answer; at multiple stages, you can have multiple answers. These may vary depending on your family background, responsibilities, ambitions, etc., but do have this conversation with yourself as often as you can. Try to get as close to your goals as possible. No one's plans will make sense unless they survive the test of time. So plan in such a way that they will survive the test of time, and if they don't, make sure you have backup plans. It's better to have a plan and not need it than to not have a plan at all.

A classic reason why I feel you should have a plan is that when you implement it in the real world, you might see it go down the drain. You need a plan so that you can watch it go down the drain and then come up with a new one along the way. That's just how it works. What has happened in the current situation is that all of us have been brainwashed into thinking that we have to make choices at that very instant. We have to know what we want to do in that moment itself. I've seen tons of people finding it difficult to admit that they don't know what's going on or where they want to go. The words "I don't know" have been the most difficult for some people to utter. This begs the question: why do we feel the need to fill this gap? Why do we say the first thing that pops into our head? It's okay to not know where you want to go. No one's holding a gun to your head to make a decision. You can take your time and figure it out. Try to have an understanding of the general direction, and if you don't have it, take the time to find it. In the meantime, you can always explore and try out different options.

In most cases, I look at situations in a threefold manner. Either I know for certain that yes, I'm in favor of this, or I know for certain that no, I'm not in favor of this, or lastly, my favourite: I don't know. In that case, I go and do the thing, and eventually, it turns into one of the first two options. You don't hold it against yourself, your ego, or anything for that matter when you look at your options this way. You can be wrong; you can be right—that's what will help you grow. Admitting your mistakes, realizing how you can mend them, and becoming a better individual are essential steps in this process.

In this particular regard, I don't blame you—not even for a second. To think on any level that it's your fault would be wrong. We are a generation that has experienced every piece of information we have ever wanted at the tip of our fingers, so it's difficult for us to fathom not having an answer at that very instant. Delayed gratification, building toward something bigger, and looking at life as a whole picture rather than with a magnified vision are concepts we don't yet have a clear grasp of. These things take time, and you'll have to actively invest your time and effort into understanding yourself. Once you feel that something might interest you, go for it. At that very instant, give it some time. Act on it in one way or another. If you don't act upon it, you'll leave it in the back of your mind until it pops up again someday, or you might not think of it at all. Five minutes of working on yourself are better than no minutes of working on yourself. It doesn't take a lot of effort. What it takes is consistency and an understanding of why you're doing it in the first place. It'll take time, but eventually, you'll get there. Most of life is supposed to be neutral. You'll have moments of happiness, and you'll have moments of sadness. In the end, you'll have a stable life. For that, you'll have to actively make micro efforts. Those tiny minutes that you dedicate to improving your mindset, your health, and your career will help build your future.

CHAPTER XI

Tech It Easy

Technology as we know it has become an irreplaceable part of our lives. The pandemic has only accelerated the encroachment of these rectangles into our daily routines. So, where does it stop? That's a question all of us should be considering. Technology isn't an evil or a monster that you have to slay. There are both good and bad parts to it, and it's important to highlight both.

Let's start with this: 'You' are the product. The sooner you understand this, the better. There are countless apps now that don't sell a product; instead, they manipulate your behavior to sell you things that benefit them. Wondering how? Ever thought about why you spend countless hours scrolling through memes on the internet? Find that doggo adorable? That's exactly where they want you—sitting in front of the screen, tapping your time away, wondering why you feel drained even though you haven't done any actual work. Don't worry; there is a solution, but we'll get to that later. This chapter is just to highlight the problem and its extent.

You need to understand that your applications are not as friendly as they might seem. Countless apps have permissions granted to your microphone. That's right—they are most definitely listening. Don't you sometimes wonder how these apps know what you like? Is it purely their guesswork? I wish. It has a lot to do with behavioral changes and constant engagement. A good way to find out where the industry is heading is by watching the documentary *The Social Dilemma* on Netflix. It showcases how these companies function to some extent.

Now, let's get back to why I decided to have this conversation with you. Consider this the beginning of a self-help group. I, too, am heavily dependent on and engrossed in technology. From one addict to another: welcome to the party, pal. Now, the real question is, are we all doomed? Not necessarily.

Think back to the good old days of your childhood. Remember how the house was full of opportunities to explore and play because your parents constantly shouted at you not to use your phone? Think about whether you could leave your phone alone for a whole day. Could you accomplish that? Would it be possible for you to just break all contact, not connect to Wi-Fi for any reason on your mobile device, and only use it for incoming and outgoing calls? Maybe use your laptop for emergencies? Under no circumstances should you use it for watching memes, videos, or any other entertainment. Can you do it? I'll leave you with a better question: if yes, what will you do with all this time on your hands?

By now, you must have given some thought to what you would do without your precious technology. If you're anything like me, you'd find yourself baffled by the ample amount of time on your hands. This is where it gets tricky. To be straight with you, I had reached a stage where I was completely blank. It had come to a point where if I didn't check my phone for notifications or watch something, I was the equivalent of a mindless blob. That's when it hit me: it's time to make a change.

So, as I mentioned earlier, think about your childhood days. What did you take joy in? You have a huge range of options. For most millennials, it was all about board games, outdoor games, puzzles, daydreaming, etc. For Gen Z, it was somewhat similar but more oriented towards technology, so don't worry—I have suggestions for you as well. Some of the things I did to make myself less addicted included only keeping notifications for the most important apps. Normal text messaging apps are the only ones that I use which have notifications; for the remaining ones, I turned them off. The other thing I managed to do was go through all the apps on my phone and change the settings. Any applications that did not need access to my microphone or camera had those permissions revoked. If you're as determined as I am on my mission, you can turn these permissions on every time you need to do a particular task and turn them off again once you're done.

Now that we have some peace and quiet, where do we go from here? Screen time. Yup, I know we've all tried at some point in our lives to reduce screen time, but here's the thing: plan around a particular event. If you do it by counting hours, you'll barely make a dent. If you plan it around an event, you'll find yourself in a better position. Food time is no-screen time. I actively avoid my phone or laptop during meals. The steps are very simple but very difficult to implement. Just keep in mind that they are necessary and for your benefit.

Once you've minimized the tech part, the next point to tackle is replacement. I started using this time to catch up with my parents, and it has proven to be very helpful. Family time is a must. Other things you can do with this extra time on your hands include painting, reading a book, playing chess, making a jigsaw puzzle, working on your mental health, or learning a language. The options are infinite. What I'm trying to tell you is that if you look at how you've been spending your time throughout the week on your rectangle, you'll find that a significant amount of it is spent absorbing and retaining garbage. You want to be able to utilize this time to better yourself, to give yourself the rest you need. Exercise, and see what wonders you can achieve by merely teching it easy.

CHAPTER XII

Capital Growth

Throughout life, you will hear the word "capital" countless times. Trust me, it might get to the point where you'll get tired of seeing the word, so bear with me. My elder brother, through his experience, guided me to start my investment journey early in my teenage years. As a rebellious kid who had the privilege of being oblivious to the world of money, I decided not to pay heed to those words of wisdom. Three years later, it hit me like a truck what those words meant. Thankfully, my father had already set me up for a good head start. The topic of financial capital got me thinking. These were my exact thoughts on the matter.

I don't believe that in life you'll only have financial capital. I believe we come across a wide variety of capitals—from career to relationships and all the way up to health. So, fasten your seatbelts because this is going to be a long ride. Let's start with career capital. We don't always know where we want to end up. Even if we do, we don't know if we'll be able to make it there. None of our decisions will make sense unless they survive the test of time. So, the best thing I would recommend is to believe that you made the right decision and have the willpower to see it through until you hit a roadblock. Don't forget to keep asking yourself whether you are going in the right direction. Are you losing your objectivity? The hardest thing for me in this regard was reaching out to people. When you have friends who are willing to help you no matter what, you need to have the courage to ask for it. Remember that in life, help and advice are only given to those who have the courage to ask for it. You will find it extremely cumbersome to make it on your own. So, be humble and don't hesitate to reach out to your friends in times of need. That's what friends are for—to be with you till the end.

Coming back to career capital, the decisions you make toward your career need to make sense in a certain way. You need to arrange and plan things in a manner that builds up to something. These would be the skills you acquire and learn over the years, the network you establish during your time. Keep in mind that life is too short to make sense, so it's okay to do radical things as long as you have the stomach to sustain through it. When you plan your career, look at the bigger picture. Trace your steps back from that point and then from where you are, building a bridge to join these two points together. In the middle of it all, you will find yourself. Work toward building what you want and have backup plans in case one of these doors closes. When you bang your head on enough doors, you tend to realize which ones are more likely to crack.

When we talk about relational capital, I think we tend to forget the most important thing in life today: the barter system. Trading one commodity for another as if they are of equal weight—that's where we are currently, the barter age, according to me. We tend to see people based on the value they hold. What matters is what people bring to the table, not the fact that they have a seat at that very table. Human connection as a whole is missing. When was the last time you interacted with someone without considering their worth? Just because they are human? This often happens in a professional environment. Make friends, build relationships, actively invest your time in people, and see the wonders it brings you. Surely, you'll have blunders, fights, and miscalculations—those are part and parcel of life. But at the end of it all, you'll know you tried. Again, bite off only what you can chew. Just remember that no amount of money in the world will help you if there aren't people to support you. The pandemic has been the best example of this scenario. We have seen the need for human connection. We are, after all, a social species. The sad part is, in today's world, your intentions are questioned when you don't have a clear ulterior motive. Regardless, take tiny steps. Trust, but verify. Do it at your own pace.

Health capital is perhaps one of the topics closest to my heart. I had the fortune of understanding the importance of health at an early age. Don't take it for granted. When you reach a certain age, you tend to look back and wonder, "How did things get so bad so quickly?" Yet we tend to ignore the toll our bodies have withstood over the years. There is no wrong time to start thinking about yourself. The right time to do it was yesterday, and the second-best time to do it is now. You don't have to go to the gym and spend countless hours working on yourself. You can make those choices along the way. Understand that everyone's body is different. Just because something worked for someone doesn't mean it will work the same way for you. Yes, certain baseline parameters are common for all of us—meditation, exercises, yoga, or whatever you feel is suitable for your body is what you should go ahead with. Dedicate five minutes of your time to your body, and watch it respond positively over time. I'm sure that once you get used to it, after building a habit, your body will actively urge you to do more. That's just how it works. Your body always tells you what it needs; the only question is, do you listen? Discipline is what you require. The earlier you move towards achieving that quality, the easier your life will be.

Finally, we come to financial capital, and this is where I leave it up to you. The objective of this book and its chapters is to present ideas to you so that you, as a reader, can decide your take on these particular topics. Inflation is on the rise. Whether you see it or not, the wheels of the economy continue to turn, and with it, your money tends to degrade in value. You must have heard someone or another complain about how things aren't as cheap as they used to be. A hundred rupees in 1985 are not equivalent to a hundred rupees today. So, it's important that all of us financially educate ourselves to understand the value of money. Financial literacy is a must, so here's my recommendation: take the time to educate yourself. You don't have to be a master at it. "Jack of all trades is a master of none, but oftentimes better than a master of one." That's the complete proverb. You just need to know where and what these things are and understand what you can do better. Talk to people, talk to your friends, talk to your parents, watch educational videos, read blogs that explain good investment methodologies. Just don't invest randomly. Learn and invest. Understand that time in the market will always beat timing the market. I'm sure you can take it up from there. Starting your investment journey early will set you on a good path for life. Make it an everyday conversation. Why do we hesitate to discuss money? Why do we want to hide it? Don't we use it on a day-to-day basis? So break down the walls and bust the myth. Just educate yourself and learn. You will do wonders.

CHAPTER XIII

Breaking the Cycle

Human beings as a species have evolved and survived through their ability to adapt. You are here because your ancestors chose to fight and prevail. It's just in your blood. What most of us fail to identify, unless it's too late, is that within our cycle of life, there's another cycle that runs in the background—a cycle that has persisted for generations.

Our families and generations have benefited us greatly. They have provided us with lessons and teachings that we carry throughout our lives. The question is: is it all just the good that you carry forward, or are there other elements you want to break out of? Think, for example, if you belong to a family of scholars who share a common love for academics—maybe you don't enjoy studying, even though you are good at it. Maybe you want to pursue other avenues. Shouldn't you be able to? The answer here is complicated. Unlike most issues, if the problem originates at home, it doesn't leave the confines of our walls. All of us contribute to the problem in one way or another. You can't just rebel your way out of it. Understand that this cycle has persisted for generations. You might hear phrases like, "We don't believe in mental health because it didn't exist during our time." This is understandable—you can't talk about something you aren't aware of or don't fully understand. Unless you have firsthand experience or someone points it out to you, how would you know? The only way to understand there are ink stains on your shirt is if someone points them out or if you look down. Quite frankly, how often do you look down? We're too busy ogling at what others have on their clothes.

So, identifying where changes need to be made is a task in itself. It's simple, but not easy. The sooner you learn that nothing in life is going to be easy, the better you'll be at coping with things. It can take a toll to break the cycle. It could be stigma, prejudice, or even malice. It needs to be a silent fight. Understand that the gentle waters of the sea shape the rocks as they make their way without creating a ruckus. There will be good things and there will be bad things. It is your decision—if you want to bring change, it needs to start with you. When you strengthen yourself internally at your own pace, only then can you reflect that change outwardly. You cannot bring calm to the world if you have a storm raging within yourself.

Take the time to build yourself up—it's something that is optional. You don't owe the world anything to sit and fix its course. Yet, if you want to understand, you can. You most definitely can. It's not just the bad things you can fix. This is a belief I've carried for quite some time: you are always equipped to face the challenges you come across. In some form or another, the answer exists—all you have to do is look hard enough. Consider that maybe your family isn't well-versed in financial literacy. There are certain guidelines your parents followed because that's what they were taught. To make a change, you have to convince them how the benefits will outweigh the current state. If you want the responsibility of making this change happen, then you need to show the courage to ask for it and, most importantly, the discipline to see it through.

The elderly people in your life have some form of wisdom. They've seen the good old days and some bad ones too. Everyone has their own share of intelligence. Sit and listen. Educate yourself. If you want to solve a problem, you need to understand it in the first place. Even basic things, from cooking and maintaining relationships to making decisions, are skills that one needs to learn. What better way to understand than by seeing how past decisions panned out? Remember, no decision will make sense unless it survives the test of time. This is where you have an advantage. Their decisions have survived through time, which is why, when they share them, you will know how to move ahead. The problem with not understanding history is that you are bound to repeat the mistakes of the past in the future. So, if you want to break the cycle, you need to put a brake on it. The only question is, where do you stop?

This isn't easy, I understand. So, don't rush—just sit and learn. Work in small amounts, but work toward making your life better. Your environment, your choices, and your close ones define who you are and who you will be. Not letting it get to you will cause some sort of stress and exhaustion. It can take years to break the cycle, but understand that those who come after you will live a better tomorrow. You and your loved ones will be better off. So, ride when you are ready, and make sure you have your helmet on.

CHAPTER XIV

Invest in Yourself

Oftentimes, we tend to forget about the one person with whom we will be spending the rest of our lives—ourself. It's quite easy to neglect our own existence. You have so much on your plate. Your mind and body have to work in coordination. You, as an individual, have to look after your health, job, family, and responsibilities—so many things, all handled by one person. How exactly will you find the time to dedicate to yourself?

That's the secret, my friend: there will never be time. You will always have to make it. Learning to say no when you don't want to say yes is a skill one must develop over time. It's extremely important that you do this while maintaining relationships. It's a tightrope walk indeed—one wrong step, and down go all your efforts. So, you will always have to make time for yourself.

The part about being an adult that I've learned is that you'll always have responsibilities. There will always be 'That' thing—you know, that thing that stops you from doing what you want? Yeah, it never stops. You will have to find a way around it. Giving yourself some time is the most crucial thing you can do. While you swim your way through this gigantic ocean of life, wouldn't you like to take some time aside to watch the sunset? Maybe pet a few dolphins along the way?

The point I'm trying to make is, while you're building toward your future, dedicate some time to build toward your future self. Tiny habits make massive impacts. Want to learn a new language, pick up a musical instrument, or start your own collection? Anything under the sun that your future self would appreciate is a blessing. You know that emptiness you feel when you don't exactly know what to do with your time? Start from there. Replace your old habits with new ones.

Do your research. If you're unsure, try whatever comes to mind. If you notice that a friend is good at something, even someone you're close to, remind them that you recognize that particular attribute. You never know who could use a gentle push or a pat on the back in a time of crisis. The problem with fighting most of our battles inwardly is that, on the outside, you rarely get to hear the battle cry—the screams, the anguish. Just as you'd want to develop good habits, you should also work on addressing your issues. Your habits of today define who you will be in the future. Who wouldn't want to live a happy life?

We've all been rewired to experience happiness as soon as possible. Through our technology, we've ensured that we get just the right dose to keep us going, but the question is, where do we go from here? When we look at the bigger picture, what is it that we see? Are you just mindlessly churning out the same old story again and again, or is there actually something new under the sun?

When I talk about investing in yourself, I mean all of you—the good and the bad. Reconcile with the mistakes you have made, appreciate the achievements you have gained, and work toward the goals you have in mind. It may take some time to get there, but sooner or later, you will. All it takes is one step forward. You can take all the rest you need; this is your journey. Your time to shine.

CHAPTER XV

In Sickness & In Health

None of us particularly enjoy being sick. It's a sad and gloomy feeling. You don't have the energy, food doesn't taste that good, and life seems as if it has lost its colour. Overall, it feels as if there's not much you can do about it. Having had my share of sickness over the years, I've realized that our beliefs toward illness are a bit skewed. I used to think that it was solely up to me to bear through the illness, but I began to realize later on that this wasn't entirely the case.

Yes, you are right; if you're sick, you're the one who bears the toll. Whatever the repercussions, you're the one who has to face them head-on. But the one factor we often overlook is the people around us. We tend to forget that those who care for us also go through the illness along with us. This brings me to an important point: sometimes we forget that our actions have an impact on the people around us. Our decisions and our condition also take a toll on those close to us.

One of the hardest things in life is watching a loved one suffer through an ailment and not knowing how to make them feel better. No one would like to be in those shoes. More often than not, we tend to ignore the people closest to us, and in the worst cases, we take them for granted. If someone gives you their time and you take them for granted, what does that make you? Well, human, to say the least, because once again, we are all at fault here. We've all been taken for granted at some point, and we've all taken someone for granted at some point. The idea I want to put across is to work on reducing this. Understand that any healthy relationship is a two-way street. What you give will come back to you. Sure, right now, you might not need people; maybe you never will. In that case, make sure you're strong enough to carry yourself on your own.

We are social animals; we always have been. We've progressed because, as a collective, we kept sharing information, passing down knowledge, ensuring that at every step of the way, no one had to sit down and start from scratch. That's how we learn; that's how we progress.

There have been people who helped you in the worst of your times. People who stood by your side when you were going through your toughest battles. Just because you emerged victorious doesn't mean you walk away with a clean slate. It is my firm belief that once someone helps you when you are in dire need, you can never fully repay them. It doesn't mean you have to be burdened by their help. It simply means that you should maintain that relationship. Acknowledge and understand that no matter how you try to repay the debt, it will never be completely cleared. It does not undo the act of kindness that was shown to you at that particular moment. Even if you do not repay it in any shape or form, learn to understand and remember. Be grateful. We tend to forget the people who were there for us through it all. So, let's try to do a better job of being there for them when they need us.

Think about it vividly—how often do you express your appreciation to a friend, a relative, or even someone close to you? I understand that our society isn't particularly expressive. Expressing words of affirmation has been a taboo subject for some reason. But why not bring about a change? Why not encourage and support the people we care about? Who doesn't like to be liked? All of us, in one way or another, do want to be liked. Be kind and respectful to whomever you can. Try to let the other person know what's going through your mind. Again, it doesn't have to be with everyone, but when it comes to people you genuinely care about, you should let them know—at your own pace.

How often do we sit down and have a talk with our parents, thanking them for the privileges they have granted us? How often do you tell a friend who is there for you through thick and thin that their presence means the world to you? These aren't disclaimers or burdens that you have to carry with you. This is a reminder that life is too short, and we tend to forget these moments that make it worth living. Sharing and expressing yourself will help you understand yourself better and, overall, make you a better individual. Isn't that what we're all working toward?

CHAPTER XVI

Relationships & You

Relationships are difficult—let's start from there. It isn't easy. The basic rule of thumb is that when two people decide to share their time, space, and attention, there will be conflicts. How you resolve or handle those conflicts is what decides the nature and fate of your relationship. What I've observed so far is that relationships are about time, effort, space, and understanding. You might have someone who is great at communicating or voicing their opinions, while on the other hand, you might have someone who feels deeply for you but isn't quite able to put it into words.

The first thing you should probably get out of your head is that your partner is the answer to all your problems. They merely supplement your life; they can't become the center of your universe. None of us are irreplaceable. We might love someone to a degree that they seem irreplaceable, but that isn't quite the case. There was a period in your life when you were happy without that person being part of it, and even if they leave, there will come a time when you will be happy again. Time is the best healer if you let it work its magic.

Once you start understanding that your partner isn't supposed to solve every single problem you encounter and that they are merely there to support you through the process, you truly begin to figure out relationships. Keep in mind that you are 50 percent of the bond you share. You can continue to work on yourself while you're with someone, or even if you need the space to work on yourself separately. It's about understanding what it is that you desire. If peace is what you long for, then peace is what you should set out to find.

There is a sense of comfort that comes with being used to someone. This is different from taking someone for granted. You know each other's strengths, so you work towards making the best of them. As I've mentioned before, you will keep changing as time passes, and so will the definition of your relationship. How you communicate is the backbone of your bond. Are you able to express yourself freely? Do you feel burdened by not being able to share things with your partner? Do you feel your voice is heard? These are just some of the many questions to consider.

This won't happen as simply as love at first sight. Love might happen at first sight, but marriages happen after the long haul. You need to give each other the benefit of the doubt, get into arguments, express your vulnerable side, deal with financial problems, loss of a loved one, and so many other challenges to know how the other person reacts. Even then, you can never truly predict how a person might turn out to be. What you do is take a chance—that this person is someone you want to be around for as long as possible, as long as it makes sense. Give yourself and your partner time to understand each other's language. Everyone has their own language, and decoding it will take time. Do whatever feels comfortable to you, and keep exploring until you find those things.

Remember, your relationships go beyond just romantic ones. You have your friends, family, colleagues, and so many others. In each of these, you can be a different person altogether, while the fundamental aspect of you remains the same. You might be different around people from your school, reminiscing about old times. You might be different when hanging out with your colleagues, probably sharing mutual pain over projects and late nights. In each of these, you may present a different side of yourself, which isn't necessarily a bad thing. You should explore yourself and the type of person you are; only then will you understand yourself better. We can always set our own priorities for these relationships. Where you want to devote your time is your personal decision. Just remember that at the end of all this, you still need to have a healthy relationship with yourself as well.

CHAPTER XVII

Tech It to the Next Level

Our modern world revolves around technology. It has become such an integral part of our day-to-day lives that it is quite difficult to completely omit it. Even when you want to, it will require a lot of effort, and more importantly, the question arises: how long would you want to continue on those lines? Detoxing is a separate thing. You take a week or so where you completely avoid technology, but the fact of the matter remains that it has already cast its shadow on our lives.

The next thing to consider is whether it's a lost cause. Has the ship already sailed? Is there no way back? Can we just abandon everything—hope lost altogether? Not really. We aren't at the grim end where everything leads to nowhere. Before you begin utilizing technology as a powerful tool, I'll give you a magic spell. The spell is simple: "There will always be more."

How much of it is enough? How many memes? How many videos? How much artwork? How many movies will it take to satisfy your hunger? There will always be more. Once you let this be your guiding light and practice it, you'll be able to use technology as a tool, use it in moderation, and effectively identify what it is that you truly desire. So, let's start the reverse journey of understanding how to use technology for our benefit.

When we talk about technology, we're often referring to popular social media platforms. The good part about your online life is that you can live as many lives as you want. You can create a life of whatever you desire. That's what got me thinking. Initially, once I signed on, I started randomly liking and saving whichever posts I wanted. It created a mess on my feed—something that all of us must have experienced. Let me explain a basic thing: the way these platforms work is to throw content at you that you will consume. So, whatever they think you'll enjoy and spend time on, they'll keep throwing your way. Based on the things you search, the posts you like, and the content you save, they'll keep recommending similar things.

Now, understand a fundamental difference: the algorithms do try to give you content from other domains because the more domains, the more likely you'll spend time on these platforms. This is where you have to show resilience. You have to display that you are not interested in particular things. Don't click on them anyway. If need be, click on do not recommend; the recommendation system heavily internally penalizes this content to ensure reduction of its mention on your feed.

Let's say you've thought of the perfect life you want to live. You're tired of watching memes and going through content that makes you feel drained, but you don't know how to end the cycle. Let's say you start a new virtual life, one where you only follow accounts that put out content about yoga, meditation, cooking, investments, trekking, language learning, mental health, and so on. This is just an example, but you will automatically find yourself surrounded by just this kind of content. How many times have you thought of starting your life over with a clean slate? This is your opportunity to live your virtual life the way you see fit. Even in these cases, remember our golden magic spell: there will always be more. So, you should be able to put down your weapon—your devices—and take the time to implement these things.

The root of all success is consistency, consistency, and consistency. If you can walk the talk—essentially, do the things you say you would—you will be happier in life. A feedback cycle will show you that with every achievement, you'll be motivated to do better. If you aren't able to do so, that's when you'll find problems with your confidence and start questioning your decisions. Set small goals and give them a try. You have in your hands a sword that can slay any monsterous goal of yours, helping you accomplish whatever you want. But remember that it, too, needs to be kept aside, sharpened, and taken care of. You can only rely on it for so long. The most important weapon for achieving your goals is you and your mindset.

CHAPTER XVIII

Hacking Yourself

We all have our set of habits and addictions, whether it's staring at the mobile screen, eating fast food, smoking, or whatever else under the sun. These cravings, addictions, and habits are what make us human. There must have been times when you've asked yourself, "Why am I like this? Why can't I quit watching series while I eat? Why can't I put down that drink? Why do I crave that drag?" We've all been there, or we know someone who has. So, how do we get rid of this feeling—the lingering emotion of wanting to quit but finding it very hard to do so? Let's take a deeper dive.

The story begins with the question: Where does it all come together? What are you trying to replace, or what are you trying to ignore? Understand that most of your cravings and addictions help you to replace certain emotions. Know that these things are designed to get you hooked, from the content you see on your phone to the sugar in your soft drinks. They don't hide it at all; it's all kept in plain sight. Everyone knows it; it's no secret. And yet, despite knowing this fact, why do we tend to fall prey to these one-time magic tricks? The answer lies deeper. It's easy to brush this off as a one-time deal—something you do because, who cares, it's just once. But how often does this "once in a lifetime" thing occur throughout the year? That's something we should all ponder. Think big.

When you start understanding your patterns, you begin to understand who you are as a person. Look at your habits and understand where they come from. These don't necessarily have to be big things; even micro-habits can make a major difference. I'll give you a simple example. I have the habit of getting too engrossed in my work. This is a perfect opportunity for my parents to remind me of the tasks I need to do. While I do pay some attention to the work they've described, I tend to forget it by the time I'm done with my work. After countless discussions about how I could forget such simple things, I reached the conclusion that something had to change. I started experimenting and finally found out what works best for me. I keep visual cues around me to remind me of the task at hand—like a cloth bag if I'm supposed to buy groceries or setting alarms for making tea. You get the point. The key here is that these reminders are tailored to my personality. I know that I hate the sound of alarms enough that I'll make it a point to remember the task before it goes off just to have the satisfaction of not letting it ring.

This is where you'll have to put in the work. Tailor things in such a way that you can hack yourself. Establish good habits. It's always better to replace a bad addiction with a good one. What's considered good or bad is purely up to you. If you decide this is how you want to be, then that's how you shall be. It all begins with looking at yourself and questioning your actions. Once you start identifying these patterns, you can begin to make changes. I try to micro-hack myself quite often these days. To do so, you'll need to get to know yourself as a person. It starts by checking your behavior and paying attention to what people say about you—again, these should be people whose opinions matter to you, people you trust. We are all in the same boat; everyone is a victim of some form of addiction. Remember, no one—and absolutely no one—can hide like an addict. This is where your honesty comes into play. If you tend to deceive yourself, you'll find it difficult to get things done in an orderly fashion. So start by being honest with yourself. Acceptance is key. You can only criticize and tweak something that's in front of you.

The most important hacking comes to your health. While other parameters are arbitrary, we often tend to ignore the basic things that make up our health. Your eyes, ears, neck, and other crucial body parts require rest as well as exercise. We wait until a symptom flares up and then question, "Boy, oh boy, where did it all go wrong?" Why not take a few minutes each morning to meditate, put your mind at ease for the day, and get enough sleep at the right time to let your body do its job of wear and tear? Why not go for a brisk walk, even if it's within the confines of your home? You can't imagine how much a 5-minute brisk walk can help you feel better. Don't wait for symptoms to show up before you take measures to reduce the damage. It's easier to have the foresight to see these problems rather than contemplate the manifestation in hindsight. Active measures help prevent the radical outcomes of the future. So what are you waiting for? Put on your thinking cap and see for yourself what you have in store for you.

CHAPTER XIX

Burnout

We've all been told at some point by an elder, a relative, or even some friends, "Just do well in this examination, and you'll be set for life." We accept it as the whole truth, perhaps even as the gospel truth on a subconscious level, and try our best to give maximum effort. But is it true? Is it so important that we are asked to cut out everything else from our lives just to focus on this one examination? Well, it's only the half truth.

This issue usually begins with our 10th board exams. They are considered the golden metric for determining whether an individual will be successful in life or not. I will never understand how one examination can define the fate of an entire life, yet this is the reality in our modern world. Many parents ensure their children have all the resources they need to secure the best marks in these exams. There's nothing wrong with wanting the best for our loved ones. The issue arises when we don't fully understand the cost at which these results are obtained.

When you are at an age where your entire worldview is shaped by the people around you, something like this creates a false image in your head. Students who go through these golden metric exams often find themselves held in high regard and are expected to repeat this "magic" in the years to come. They never seem to catch a break. What they experience is burnout—a vicious cycle of realizing that they pushed themselves to the limit to get good results in exams they thought were the most important, only to find they have no energy left to continue. That's where the half-truth comes in.

I, too, was misinformed in this case. I assumed I had to put all my energy—everything I had—into this one examination, and after that, I wouldn't have to worry about anything in life. I did secure a good score, but the issue was that more exams followed. Remember, there will always be more exams to follow. The way I see these exams is as an introduction to the world. If you do well, your confidence is boosted, your parents' faith in you is strengthened, and you carry that forward. Even if you score less or fail, you learn a valuable lesson: regardless of whether you do well or poorly, there will always be someone who questions your actions. There is no limit to how long that discussion will drag on. If you score in the 80s, you'll always be asked why you didn't score higher. Even if you get a well-paying job, someone will always compare you to a peer who seems to be doing better. This comparison charade will never cease. So yes, it is a valuable lesson to carry on in life. No matter what you do, if you let others be the sole judge, they will always have the last word.

The real story begins when you secure a score you thought was good enough. Once you prove yourself and set a certain standard, people only expect you to go higher. This will always be taxing if you don't know how to cope with the added pressure. Deep down, you might feel that pulling off your "magic" again will take so much more effort. We've all seen examples of this—stories of individuals studying day and night with nothing else on their minds. The funny part is that since I thought my 10th grade marks were the sole criteria for defining success, I assumed that the higher the score, the better the individual. But that's not even close to the truth. I knew people who scored lower than I did, yet I was sure they were more talented. It was when I was preparing for my JEE Advanced exams that this illusion finally shattered. I saw people who scored less than me doing better in the mocks. When I asked how they were doing so, I was told that some of them had been studying since their 8th standard.

So you get the idea. We've all been told that this is a sprint, a one-time deal, but in reality, it's a marathon. So, is it all a lie? Is there no reason to study hard or work hard? That's what we'll talk about now. When people tell you that you need to work hard so you are set for life, they are only half-right. You might be set for that portion of your life. Let me elaborate. Let's go back to the boards. If you do well, you gain confidence, and you go on to a better college. You do well in the next exam, and you get into a better college for your undergraduate degree. All these things matter—where you study, what projects you work on, what type of folks you hang out with, how much you work on yourself. Every bit of it matters. What you need to understand is that at every step, you must maintain momentum. The only way to avoid burnout is by maintaining consistency. It's all about knowing when to work hard and when to actively take time off for yourself, giving yourself the rest you need to recuperate, and jumping back into the ring. You need to detach and reattach in the right proportion in order to be consistent.

If you don't do well at any point in this cycle, it doesn't mean it's over for you. All it means is that you'll have to work harder in the next part of your life's journey—maybe twice or three times as hard as your peers. Know the fact that for the ones who did well, they get opportunities more easily; their chances of getting success become higher, and yours automatically don't become zero. The day you convince yourself that you are doomed is when the downward trend shall follow. What you need to understand is that this isn't a competition between you and your friends or peers. It's a journey of finding the things you want to do and working towards that goal. So, keep in mind that comparing yourself to your peers will only instill jealousy and hatred.

So make sure to take that active break, make sure to set boundaries, hold yourself accountable, yet make time for the things you love. Only then will you be able to live a more wholesome, fulfilled life; otherwise, you'll be stuck in this perpetual cycle of looking for external validation, which will leave you with a sense of emptiness. The idea here is to focus on what you love, let it mindfully drive you, bit by bit make you whole, and give you the satisfaction of a life well spent.

CHAPTER XX

Maze of Life

Imagine you have in front of you a map that leads to a treasure that will sustain you and your generations for life. You look across the sea and quickly begin to think about how you will travel to acquire this hidden treasure. The winds blow calmly, and the sea feels welcoming, but you aren't quite able to fully understand what the map indicates. The language and symbols appear to be encoded. Bursting through the door, you grab a chair and sit down by the study, determined to figure out what it could possibly mean.

Having some sense of the general direction to move towards, you instruct the crew on the journey ahead. One thing is clear: It's going to take a long time to acquire this hidden wealth. It doesn't matter, you tell yourself; as long as you know it exists, you will set sail across the seas to make it yours. You travel for days and finally reach your first destination. In the middle of the night, you light up a torch and set foot on the sandy beach. The sky, lit with stars, marks this beautiful moment. You decide to rest for a couple of hours until the sun rises. In your head, only one thought runs: I must do everything it takes to get what I want. Even though the map seems as confusing as ever, you feel confident that you will get what is yours.

In the morning, you begin your exploration of the island. With everything on your person—your backpack, swords, and the map—you head into the forest. It takes you weeks to figure out the ins and outs of the place. Thankfully, there are no predators on this land. Food is plentiful, and drinking water is available; you could build your life right here and be happy.

"Am I even in the right place?" is a constant thought that goes through your mind. Exhausted, you lay in your cave wondering what the map could mean when it finally strikes you. Like a spark that kindles a fire, you quickly start orienting the map in different directions. Cumbersome as the task may be, you find yourself spending hours making sense of it until a clearer picture begins to form. "I read it wrong! I'm in the complete opposite direction," you finally realize. You had interpreted it incorrectly, so you begin to pack up your belongings and head back to your ship. You have months of travel ahead of you. "Is it even going to be worth it?" a question runs across your mind.

"I'm here now; this is the best I've ever lived. I can make something of my own here, but I need to explore more. I can always return if I feel like it," you conclude. And so it begins—the worst of your times. Amidst the journey, you find yourself in raging storms and lightning. It's a miracle if you make it to a safe location. With every impact from the angry waters, you take your time to mend your ship. Hope is lost at times, and you take the opportunity to rest, recoup, and set sail again. Finally, after months of endeavor, you find yourself at your desired location. This time, you are sure you are in the right place. You and your crew are ready for whatever lies ahead. It is no secret that the land is not safe. Tons of predators, wild plants, and dangers await you. This is the time you decide to split up and explore. "Within a week, we shall all meet back here to discuss our findings," you instruct.

After a week, some of them return, and that's when it hits you that maybe some lost their way... maybe they didn't make it. Unsure of what might have happened, you convince yourself that you have to continue. You sit down and discuss with everyone what they found. With the help of the others, you come to realize that each group had a different experience on the island. It led to the discovery of the dangerous animals, poisonous plants, and most importantly, where the first artifact might be—at the top of the mountain, everyone concludes.

You start scaling the mountain, a rigorous and cumbersome climb. When you finally make it to the summit, you find the artifact—a glass orb. Something clicks in your head, and you look at the map through the glass orb. The picture begins to shift, and a smile spreads across your face. Curious, your crew members ask, "What is it? What did you find?" "It changed the whole thing. It's a completely different map," you say as you plan to set out to sea once again.

Distractions, distractions, and distractions. Our modern life is such that distractions are everywhere. Building up towards something and working to get there is a difficult task. It's easier to convince ourselves that every day we do something, but unsure of what it amounts to in the bigger picture, we tend to ignore the effect of time. Time is what you have, and time is what can change the game. Currently, we have everything we need. The internet has answers to all your questions. The problem is, it also has a set of traps. Chase down the wrong rabbit hole, and you'll find yourself going down a completely different path. This is where you'll need to train your mindset to discern what is right and what is wrong. In some cases, you'll have to reach out to your friends, family, and close ones. You will have to find answers sometimes all by yourself. In some cases, you'll be enticed by the melodies of the mermaids, and in others, it just won't make sense. This is the time when your willpower and dedication will help you overcome the hurdles ahead.

The modern maze of life is one that has multiple entries and multiple exits. There isn't just one treasure lying in store for you; there are many. Understand that as you go on this path of discovery, you will experience heartbreak, you will face hardships, you will lose, and you will gain. The idea is to understand what you hold dear and fight tooth and nail to achieve it. Nothing comes easy, and whatever comes easy comes with a cost. Think about a simple exercise: Let's say you want to learn to read a new language—not speak it, just read it. You have at your disposal tons of content. Unless you put in the effort to build a habit of reading, watching videos, and understanding how to read and in what sequence, you'll never be able to get the job done. In some cases, you might just give up, which is also okay if you can make your peace with it. If not, you can take a break to energize and get back to it again. Your mental, physical, and emotional health plays a huge role in this journey.

The path to achieving your goals is laden with distractions, hurdles, and compromises. To accomplish them, you will have to bring about changes in yourself—some fundamental, some superficial. Change is the only constant. Being able to discern which sources to trust and which to ignore is a skill you'll develop over the years. No one has it figured out completely. You will have to take calculated risks to get there. Nothing will make sense unless it survives the test of time. So, the best you can do is keep exploring until you feel you have given it your best, and then try a different approach. The more effort you put in and the more you re-route your path upon failure, the more likely you are to meet your goals. The world around you may crumble to ashes, but you should have the willpower to build it again, brick by brick. Mistakes happen, failures happen. Every successful person in this world has had their fair share of failures. They learn, they accept, and they move on. So can you.

The good part about success is that it is subjective. Someone can find their peace on the shore of a beach, relaxing without worrying about any financial problems, while someone else can find it in a lavish lifestyle. There are no winners here; what we have here are people. People can wish and long for whatever they want. These parameters of success can change with time, which is again completely understandable. With relationships, with loss, with time, things will change, and so will you. What will remain constant is how you perceive and tackle things. That takes years to work on, and that's what you should do. When you enter the maze of life, you get to pick whatever you want as your prize. It matters to you to pick what is meaningful. Life is like a wish-fulfilling tree, provided you let it be, but remember, everything comes at a price. So I'll leave you with one final thought: there is no single key to success; there is only you.

About The Cover

For me, yellow has always been a sign of love. It's been my favourite colour ever since I was a child—a colour that exudes hope, peace, and calm, much like sunsets stretching across cities. Yellow reminds me of golden hours spent by the beaches of Mumbai, Bordi, Goa, and many others, moments that hold a special place in my heart.

Growing up, yellow and I formed an unusual bond. I often heard the phrase "yellow yellow dirty fellow," and it always felt unfair—like the colour was misunderstood. In a way, it mirrored how I felt about myself. I wasn't considered the smartest in the family, and there weren't many who believed I could achieve much. Like a "black sheep," I didn't show obvious signs of capability, and as a child unfamiliar with self-validation, I relied heavily on external acknowledgment, which often felt absent.

But whenever I looked at yellow, I saw something different: a colour that stood out, vibrant and pretty, despite how others dismissed it. Yellow seemed to understand me, just as I understood it. We were both underestimated, yet full of potential waiting to be seen. Over time, my connection with yellow grew stronger—it became a quiet companion, a symbol of resilience and hope, reminding me to embrace my individuality, no matter what others thought.

The sunflower, prominently featured on the cover, is a perfect representation of this journey. Sunflowers are known to turn toward the sun, seeking light even in the darkest times. They symbolize positivity, strength, and unwavering faith. Much like my fondness for yellow, I've always loved flowers for their beauty and quiet strength, and the sunflower stands as a beacon of hope and warmth—a reminder to keep growing and thriving, regardless of the odds.

Of course, I share a special bond with other colours too—they each hold a unique and cherished place in my heart. However, Yellow isn't just a colour for me; it's a part of my story. It's a reminder to look for the light, to embrace what makes me different, and to find peace in the journey.

www.ingramcontent.com/pod-product-compliance
Lightning Source LLC
Chambersburg PA
CBHW020501160726
47991CB00007B/2752